# AUTHENTIC JAPANESE
# CUISINE for beginners
## Sabi Shinojima

GRAPH-SHA/Japan Publications

# CONTENTS

### Japanese Fundamentals

MEASURES: Unless otherwise noted,
1 cup is 200 cc; 1 Tbsp (tablespoon) is
15 cc; 1 tsp (teaspoon) is 5 cc.
MICROWAVE: Microwave cooking
times are for a 600-watt oven.

About the Author:

Sabi Shinojima, daughter of
renowned cooking specialist
Chu Shinojima, first began
learning about Japanese
cooking techniques from her
father. She continued studying
Japanese cuisine in college and
soon was teaching classes at
Chu Shinojima's cooking
academy while also contributing
recipes to national newspapers
and magazines. In this volume,
she draws on her thorough
understanding of the chemistry
of cooking to reveal
professional tips, secrets, and
special techniques to beginners.
She enjoys fishing, scuba
diving, and pottery (the serving
dishes shown on page 10 and
14 are her own creations). Her
many other books in Japanese
include "Fish Slicing and
Cooking" and "160 Bento
Recipes"

# Before You Begin

## Cutting Safely

Hold the handle of the knife firmly. Rest your thumb on the handle or on the flat of the blade. Form a cat's paw with your fingers to hold the ingredient. Move your hand to the left after each cut. The two common hand positions at bottom right are unsafe.

To peel something in your hand, press your right thumb on the part that is to be cut. The blade follows the thumb, underneath the peel.
To remove the eyes from potatoes, use the bottom corner of the blade. Place your right index finger next to the eye to control the blade and avoid cutting too deeply.

## Measuring

Correct sizes are very important for Japanese cuisine. Measuring becomes much simpler if you use your own hands instead of a ruler. Try each of the positions at right with your own hand and note the results. (Figures in parentheses are for an average Japanese woman's hand.)

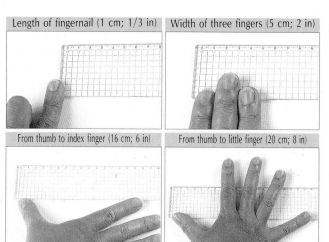

Length of fingernail (1 cm; 1/3 in)
Width of three fingers (5 cm; 2 in)
From thumb to index finger (16 cm; 6 in)
From thumb to little finger (20 cm; 8 in)

## Heating

Even when high heat is called for, do not allow flames to extend beyond the bottom of the pot. Gas is wasted and handles can be scorched.

# Chapter 1

The Ultimate Comfort Food

# Simmered Dishes

Japanese-style simmering is the ideal method to bring out the pure, cleansing flavor of vegetables. Some of the popular techniques in this chapter: *fukume-ni*, where every ingredient gets its own flavoring; *itame-ni*, where the ingredients are first sautéed before the dashi is added; and *shime-ni*, where multiple flavorings are cooked together until the liquid is absorbed.

*Left to right:* Sweet-Simmered Pumpkin; Simmered Bok Choy (p. 8).

# Simmered Bok Choy *(photo: p. 7)*

Simmer in *happoji*.

*[4 servings]*
2 bunches baby bok choy
1½ cups dashi stock
2½ Tbsp mirin
2½ Tbsp soy sauce
•This 8:1:1 proportion of dashi to mirin to soy sauce is known in Japanese as *happoji*.

**Blanch.**
1. Cut an X in base of each bok choy Boil in salted water.

2. When tender, cool in cold water, then rinse. Squeeze well; split along the Xs.

**Simmer.**
3. Boil the dashi and mirin, then add soy sauce. Add bok choy; cook briefly. Cool.

•**If soy sauce is added too soon, it gets sharp.**

# Sweet-Simmered Pumpkin *(photo: p. 7)*

Salt at the finish completes the flavor. Kabocha squash is similar to pumpkin and to acorn squash but with edible skin.

*[4 servings]*
¼ to ⅓ kabocha squash
4 cups dashi
½ cup mirin
½ cup sugar
1 tsp salt
•Dashi, mirin, and sugar—8:1:1 ratio.

**Slice kabocha.**

1. Cut into wedges; remove seeds. Cut each into 4-5 pieces.
2. Bevel the edges of the pieces.
•**Bevels prevent crumbling.**

**Simmer.**
3. Boil kabocha in dashi, mirin, and sugar. Cook for 10-15 min. on medium. When easily pierced, add salt. Cool.
•**Use a metal skewer; bamboo can crack squash.**

Use Kombu-Bonito Dashi for most dishes; Kombu for vegetarian dishes; Dried Fish for miso soup and noodle broth.

Kombu: *rishiri kombu* or *rausu kombu*. Do not use *Nikko kombu* — meant for simmered kombu rolls.

Shaved bonito: fresh. Use plenty. Keep container sealed well.

Dried fish: use new packages, if oily to the touch, discard.

## Kombu Dashi

*[for 6 cups]*
5 in (12 cm) kombu
6 cups water

1. Wipe surface with a well-squeezed wet cloth *(figure)*.
2. Add water. Let stand overnight. Remove the kombu.

•Do not cut slits. Flavor is on surface; cuts release sliminess and odor.

# Kombu-Bonito Dashi

*[for 6 cups]*
5 in (12 cm) kombu
2 cups shaved bonito
6 cups water

1. Wipe kombu with a damp towel. Heat water, then add kombu (Fig. 1). Raise heat to high.

2. When tiny bubbles form, remove kombu (Fig. 2).
•Warm water is best for kombu. Boiling water releases odor.

3. When boiling, add bonito (Fig. 3). Remove from heat. Let bonito sink.

•Hot water is best for bonito, but if it boils, it will get cloudy.

4. Strain through cloth (Fig. 4). Gently press liquid through.

•Do not squeeze. The dashi will become cloudy.

# Dried Fish Dashi

*[for 6 cups]*
15-20 g niboshi (dried sardines)
6 cups water

1. Remove heads and gizzards (Fig. 1).

2. Rub gently in a dry cloth (Fig. 2) to flake off scales, tails, and other small bits (Fig. 3). Soak larger pieces in the water overnight. Strain.

# Using Instant Dashi

Instant dashi (dashi-no-moto) is convenient for steamed-egg dishes, but its cloudiness and intensity need to be reduced:

Boil 6-7 cups water. Add 2 tsp instant dashi. Boil 1 min. Spoon off foam. Remove from heat; let settle 2-3 min. Use the clear broth; discard cloudy part.

# Simmered Bamboo Shoots

The perfect dish for spring. The *fukume-ni* method brings out the fragrance and sweetness of fresh bamboo shoots.

*[4 servings]*
2 fresh bamboo shoots
3-4 dried Japanese chilies
1-2 cups rice bran (nuka)
1½ cups dashi
2½ Tbsp mirin
2½ Tbsp soy sauce

•Stock, mirin, and soy sauce are in the traditional 8:1:1 ratio.

**Boil.**

1. Scrub the bamboo shoots well. Slice off the top ⅓ at an angle. Make vertical slits in the shoot, deeper at bottom. Trim off bottom in 4 beveled cuts.

Boil for an hour in plenty of rice bran, then cool 24 hours, to remove bitterness.

2. Boil the shoots, rice bran, and chilies in plenty of water.

**•Chilies bring out sweetness. Use unbroken ones—heat stays inside chili.**

4. Peel under running water. Use a wooden chopstick to scrape off excess.

**•Tender top layer salad: *see bottom right.***

7. Boil dashi and mirin and add soy sauce. Add shoots and cook for 3-4 min. Cool in liquid. Remove with slotted spoon and serve.

Cover the entire surface with rice bran. If rice bran is unavailable, boil in cloudy water saved from rinsing rice.

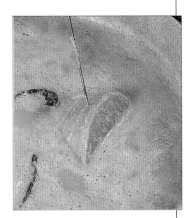

3. Lower heat. Simmer until a metal skewer easily pierces the flesh (1 hr.). Cool 24 hours in cooking liquid.

**•Bitterness leaches out into the water. Do not remove until cooled.**

5. Cut in half. Use toothpick to remove white grains. Rinse.

**•White grains are hard and chalky.**

**Simmer.**

6. Cut each piece in half. Slice each top piece into 4 wedges.
**•Use bottoms in Bamboo Rice, p. 33.**

Also Try: # Tendershoot Salad

Slice 5 oz (150 g) layers from top of a bamboo shoot into thin strips. Soften ⅓ oz (10 g) of wakame (p. 59) and chop. Serve with a ball of minced umeboshi and soy sauce.

*11*

Use at least 2 Tbsp of vinegar for every 2 cups of water.

Vinegar water whitens and sweetens. Try with burdock or lotus root.

# Simmered Udo

Udo (the white stalk of a plant similar to asparagus) has a unique fragrance. Here, the udo slowly absorbs the flavor while cooling in the pot. Udo is hard to obtain outside Japan; try using celery, white asparagus, or fennel.

*[4 servings]*
1 stalk udo
⅔ cup dashi
1 Tbsp mirin
1 Tbsp light soy sauce
Rice vinegar (for soaking)

**Prepare the udo.**
1. Fill a bowl with water and vinegar.

2. Cut udo into 2 in (5 cm) lengths. Peel. Drop into the vinegar water.
· **Peel thickly—udo is fibrous.**

3. Slice into thin strips and return to the vinegar water. Boil the udo and vinegar water. Drain; rinse in fresh water.
· **Vinegar water whitens the udo.**

**Simmer**
4. Return udo to pot with dashi, mirin, and soy sauce. Boil, then let cool in the liquid.

12

# Simmered Taro Root

Rub the taro with salt, then boil in three changes of water.

Taro is boiled first and stickiness is rubbed off before the flavors are added. To check for doneness, use a metal skewer.

[4 servings]
12 taro roots
1 heaping Tbsp salt
3 cups dashi
½ cup mirin
2 Tbsp sugar
½ cup soy sauce
8 snow peas, steamed

**Parboil the taro.**
1. Trim ends of each taro. Peel with six rounded vertical cuts. Rub with salt in a bowl. Rinse well.

2. Place the taro in a single layer in a large pot. Cover with water and bring to a boil. Remove from heat. Add cold water, then rub off the stickiness, rinse, and drain.

3. Repeat step 2.

4. Add more water to the pot and boil until easily pierced by a metal skewer. Rinse.

**Simmer.**
5. Boil dashi, mirin, and sugar, then add soy sauce and taro. Cover with wet rice paper (p. 21).

6. Reduce heat and simmer 5 min. Let cool in the liquid.

Top left: rubbing salted taro in the bowl. Top right: rubbing the boiled taro in the pot.

## Also Try: Frozen Taro

Bring an 8:1:1:1 ratio of dashi, soy sauce, mirin, and sugar to a boil. Add frozen taro. Simmer over medium heat 2–3 min. Cook on low until heated through. Cool.

# Sweet-Simmered Vegetables

Cook with plenty of sugar and mirin, then add the soy sauce.

In this traditional dish, the sweet and salty liquids are completely absorbed by the vegetables, giving them a lovely sheen. The dish keeps well in the refrigerator for up to 4–5 days and is frequently served at festive occasions.

[5 servings]
1 konnyaku (devil's-tongue jelly)
1 carrot
1 gobo (burdock root)
10 dried shiitake
1 cooked/canned bamboo shoot
1 piece lotus root
1 cup sugar
1 cup mirin
5 cups dashi
½ cup soy sauce
3 snow peas, steamed

**Prepare the ingredients.**
1. Bring konnyaku to a boil in water. After 5 min., rinse.
·**For best flavor, put konnyaku in the pot before heating.**

2. Reconstitute shiitake in warm water under a plate (p. 59).

**Slice.**

3. Konnyaku: 10 squares. Shiitake: remove stems. Bamboo shoot: remove white particles and chop. Lotus root: ⅓ in (1 cm) half circles. Carrots: chop. Gobo: 2 in (5 cm) lengths.

**Simmer.**

4. Place the gobo first; konnyaku; shiitake; carrot and lotus root; bamboo shoot last.
·**Heavy pieces on the bottom; flavor enhancers in middle; delicate pieces on top.**

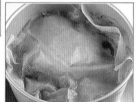

5. Add the sugar and mirin, then dashi to cover. Bring to a boil. Skim off foam. Cover loosely or with wet rice paper. Simmer 30–40 min.

The sugar softens the ingredients; the mirin prevents disintegration.

6. Add the soy sauce and simmer 10–15 min. more.

7. When the liquid is very low, shake the pot to turn its contents over. Serve with the snow peas.

# Pork and Potatoes

Cook the potatoes in the flavorings, then stir in the pork.

No dashi is needed because the meat makes its own stock.

*[4 servings]*
4 potatoes
1 onion
1 in (3 cm) carrot
7 oz (200 g) thinly sliced pork
3 cups water
5 Tbsp sugar
½ cup mirin
½ cup soy sauce
2 green beans
Salt for boiling

**Slice.**

1. Quarter the potatoes and soak in cold water.
**·The starch soaks off, preventing disintegration.**

2. Slice the onion. Julienne the carrot. Chop the pork.

**Simmer.**
3. Boil the potatoes, water, sugar, mirin, and soy sauce.

4. When boiling, stir in the pork. Spoon off the foam.
**·Waiting until the boil avoids excess foam.**

5. Simmer about 20 min. on medium until the potatoes are soy-sauce colored. Stir in the onion and cook 2-3 min.
**·Delay the onion to avoid odors.**

6. Add the carrot, stir briefly, and remove from heat. Let stand in liquid. Serve with boiled salted green beans.

Add the flavorings before heating, for best absorption.

Also Try: **Beef and Potatoes**

*[4 servings]*
In western Japan (Kyoto and points west), this dish is made with beef. Use 7 oz (200 g) thinly sliced *beef* instead of the pork. Increase *carrot* to 1½ in (5 cm). Reduce *sugar* to 3 Tbsp. Reduce mirin to ⅓ cup. Use ⅓ cup *light soy sauce* instead of the soy sauce.
1. Slice as in steps 1 and 2, but chop the carrots instead of julienne.
2. Follow steps 3-6, substituting the peas for the green beans.

# Chicken Medley

## Sauté the gobo first and the chicken will not stick to the pot.

This combination of crunchy textures is the perfect representative of *itame-ni*, where the ingredients are sautéed before simmering.

[4 servings]
½ chicken thigh
½ piece lotus root
½ carrot
½ gobo (burdock root)
1 chikuwa (grilled fish-cake tube)
½ cooked/canned bamboo shoot
3 fresh shiitake
½ cup sugar
½ cup mirin
½ cup soy sauce
3 Tbsp vegetable oil
Snow peas, steamed

・The sugar, mirin, and soy sauce are in a 1:1:1 ratio.

**Slice.**

1. Remove the fat with the tip of your knife. Cut into bite size, skin side up.

2. Quarter the lotus root and slice ⅓ in (1 cm) thick. Quarter the carrot lengthwise and chop. Chop the gobo, chikuwa, bamboo shoot, and shiitake.
**・Match the sizes for even cooking.**

**Sauté.**
3. Sauté the gobo in the oil. When coated, stir in the chicken.

4. Stir in the carrot, bamboo shoot, lotus root, and chikuwa.

**Simmer.**

5. Cover with water (3 cups) and add the sugar and mirin. When boiling, skim the foam, add the soy sauce, and cook on medium for 20 min.
**・Remove chicken fat with foam.**

Meat sometimes sticks to the pot when sautéing. The gobo cools the oil slightly, keeping the meat from sticking.

6. Add the shiitake and heat through. Slice the snow peas and scatter atop.

# Simmered White Fish with Onion

Early spring, when onions send up their shoots, is also the tastiest time of year for cooked onions. Sea bream is the perfect match for the season.

*[four servings]*
2 pieces white fish (sea bream, snapper, cod)
1 onion
1½ cups dashi
1 Tbsp sugar
3 Tbsp mirin
3 Tbsp light soy sauce

**Slice.**
1. Halve the fish pieces. Slice the onion ¼ in (6 mm) thick.
**Simmer.**

2. Bring the dashi, sugar, and mirin to a boil, then add the soy sauce. When boiling, add the fish.
•**Place the fish skin side up to avoid breakage.**

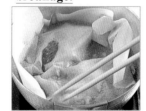

3. Spoon some of the hot broth over the exposed parts of the fish. Cover with paper and simmer 5–10 min.

4. Discard the paper and remove the fish. Add the onions and replace the fish on top. Heat through.

The surface of the fish is sealed with the heat. Avoid stirring or turning the delicate fish.

Japanese Fundamentals
•Paper Lids

The traditional wooden lid placed inside the pot (otoshibuta) is too heavy for delicate ingredients. Tuck a wet circle of rice paper or parchment paper over the fish.

Boil off all the liquid for an intense flavor
and crisp texture.

# Burdock Kimpira

The traditional
combination of
burdock root and
carrot. Be sure to
julienne them
equally.

*[4 servings]*
½ burdock root
2 in (5 cm) carrot
1 Tbsp cooking oil
3 Tbsp sugar
4 Tbsp sake
4 Tbsp soy sauce
Roasted sesame seeds
(for garnish)

•The sugar, sake, and
soy sauce are in a
3:4:4 ratio.

**Slice.**
1. Scrub the burdock
well and julienne
into 2in (5cm)
lengths. Julienne the
carrot to match.

**Sauté.**

2. Sauté the burdock
and carrot over high
heat.
•**Sauté well for a
crisp texture—or
the vegetables will
melt.**

3. Stir in the sugar,
sake, and soy sauce
and cook until the
liquid evaporates.

# Asparagus Kimpira

All varieties of
Kimpira can be
cooked ahead and
eaten cold. In this
updated version,
asparagus is spiced
with Japanese
peppers.

*[4 servings]*
6 large spears
asparagus
1 Tbsp cooking oil
2 Tbsp sake
2 Tbsp soy sauce
Seven-spice powder
(shichimi togarashi)
Roasted sesame seeds
(for garnish)

•The sake and soy
sauce are in a 1:1
ratio.

**Slice.**
1. Cut the asparagus
into ¼ in (5 mm)
diagonals. Leave the
tips whole.

**Sauté.**
2. Sauté the
asparagus until it
softens. Cook off
any liquid it
releases.

3. Add the soy sauce
and sake and stir
over high heat until
they evaporate.
•**Low heat leads to
more liquid.**

4. Add the spices.

Top: Burdock Kimpira; Bottom: Asparagus Kimpira

# Simmered Daikon with Crab

Daikon (long white radish) is most delicious in winter. Gently simmered rounds of daikon (*furofuki daikon*) are a luxurious treat on a cold day. Here, the daikon is served with a crab sauce and garnished with citron peel.

*[4 servings]*
6 in (16 cm) daikon
½ cup rice
Dashi to cover
Dash salt
4¼ oz (120 g) cooked crab meat
1 cup dashi
¼ cup mirin
3 Tbsp light soy sauce
1 Tbsp cornstarch
Citron or lemon peel

### Cut the daikon.

1. Cut the daikon into 4 rounds; peel.

### Boil with rice.

2. Boil daikon and rice in water to cover until easily pierced by a pin (15–20 min.). Rinse, then soak in cold water.
·**The rice removes the bitterness and adds sweetness.**

### Simmer.

3. Bring the daikon to a boil in dashi to cover. Add the salt and cook 10 min. over low heat.

### Make the sauce.

4. Boil 1 cup dashi, mirin, soy sauce, and cornstarch. When it thickens, add crab.
·**If something else will cook in the liquid, dissolve and add cornstarch last.**

5. Spoon the sauce over the daikon.

Blanching methods to match the ingredient.

*Water*
Start potatoes and konnyaku (devil's-tongue jelly) in cold water; the bitterness will be released as the water heats.

*Water + Rice Lees + Chile Pepper*
The lees draw out the bitterness and the chile pepper adds sweetness. Use plenty of lees for bamboo shoots.

*Water + Rice*
Bring daikon to a boil with a handful of rice to remove bitterness and heighten sweetness.

*Cold/Hot Water + Vinegar*
For lotus root, burdock root, udo, and other white vegetables, boil with vinegar.

*Hot Water + Salt*
For subtly seasoned vegetables, add the salt after the water is boiling. Salt added too soon prolongs the boiling process and sharpens the flavor.

# Chapter 2

# Rice
# Soups
# Noodles

Rice is the staple of Japanese cuisine In this chapter, we introduce the traditional ways to prepare rice on festive occasions; delicious soups to accompany any rice meal; and ever-popular noodle dishes for all seasons.

Scattered Sushi (pp. 28–29)

# Scattered Sushi (Chirashizushi) *(photo: p. 27)*

A festive dish. The many ingredients need to be placed carefully to show off their variety.

**[6 servings]**
4 rice measures (scant 3 cups; 720 cc) rice
3/4 oz (25 g) kampyo (dried gourd strips)
5 dried shiitake
*Simmering sauce*
½ cup dashi
3½ Tbsp sugar
3½ Tbsp mirin
3½ Tbsp soy sauce
*Sushi vinegar*
¾ cup rice vinegar
5 Tbsp sugar
1 Tbsp salt
4 Tbsp roasted sesame seeds
½ narutomaki (fish cake with spiral pattern)
8 prawns
Omelet Strands (one recipe, p. 53), cut into ⅛ in (3 mm) strips
Roasted nori, slivered
Salt

•For the gourd and shiitake, the ratio of dashi: sugar: mirin: soy sauce is 2:1:1:1.

Wooden sushi barrels absorb the excess moisture in the rice. If unavailable, use a large, shallow baking dish.

**Steam the rice.**
1. Rinse and drain the rice. Add water as directed and steam in a rice cooker.

**Cook shiitake and kampyo.**
2. Reconstitute the shiitake and kampyo as on p. 59 and on p. 67 respectively.

3. Boil the simmering sauce ingredients; add the shiitake and kampyo; cook until the liquid evaporates. Let stand.

**Make sushi rice.**
4. Stir the sugar and salt into the vinegar.

5. Empty the hot rice into the damp barrel. Drizzle with the seasoned vinegar.
•**Use a rice paddle to spread the stream.**

6. Stir with a cutting motion.

•**To avoid crushing the rice, use a damp cloth to push it off the paddle.**

7. When evenly blended, use a fan to cool the rice.
•**Fanning lends a gloss to the rice.**

8. When the rice reaches skin temperature, push it to one side and drape with a damp cloth.
•**The rice must stay warm or it will be difficult to mix.**

**Mince and stir.**

9. Squeeze the liquid from the shiitake and kampyo and mince. Fold into the rice with sesame seeds.

**Scatter.**

10. Slice the narutomaki into ¼-in-thick (7mm) matchsticks.

11. Devein the shrimp with a bamboo skewer. Boil in salted water until they curl. Remove the shell except for the tail.

12. Scatter the rice with the omelet strips, then with the other ingredients.

Also Try: **Box Sushi**

*[4 servings]*
1. Follow steps 1-9 to prepare the rice.
2. Prepare Egg Sprinkles (p. 53).
3. Line pan with plastic wrap. Scatter 3 chopped artificial crab legs and 3 chopped blanched green beans. Press with egg sprinkles (Fig 1).
4. Press the sushi rice on top, filling to the corners.
5. Invert. Slice through wrap with damp knife (Fig. 2). Remove wrap. Garnish with marinated ginger.

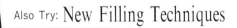

## Also Try: New Filling Techniques

### Inside–Out Rolls

Turn the tofu puff inside out and fill as usual.

### Triangle Rolls

Cut the tofu puffs on the diagonal and fill as usual.

# Inari–zushi

Roll with a rolling pin to detach the sides and make the puffs easier to open.

Ask for flawless tofu puffs (aburage) to prevent tearing. Also, use the thick end of the chopsticks to handle the puffs.

*[4 servings]*
4 rice measures (3 scant cups; 720 cc) rice
¾ cup rice vinegar
5 Tbsp sugar
1 Tbsp salt
8 tofu puffs (aburage)
2 cups dashi
½ cup sugar
½ cup mirin
½ cup soy sauce
Plum–vinegared ginger (for garnish)

•The stock, sugar, mirin, and soy sauce ratio is 4:1:1:1.

1. Rinse the rice and steam as usual. Cut in the vinegar mixture as on p. 28 (steps 4–8).

**Simmer tofu puffs**
2. Cut each tofu puff in two. Roll with a rolling pin and open.

3. To remove the oil, dip into boiling water with the thick end of your chopsticks. Press on a strainer.
•**Squeezing by hand leads to rips and burns.**

4. Bring the dashi, mirin, and sugar to a boil. Add the soy sauce and return to the boil. Add the opened puffs. Put a plate on the puffs; simmer 10 min. on medium.

5. Arrange on a strainer and press again with a wooden lid as in step 3.

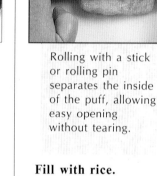

Rolling with a stick or rolling pin separates the inside of the puff, allowing easy opening without tearing.

**Fill with rice.**

6. Shape the rice into a bullet and insert it into the puff. Press one side of the opening into the rice and fold the other side over. Scatter with leaves and the ginger.

# One-Pot Rice Casserole

For even cooking, arrange the ingredients on top of the rice rather than stirring them in.

When other ingredients are steamed with the rice, the amount of water does not change. Think of the sake and soy sauce as the simmering liquid for the vegetables.

[4 servings]
4 rice measures (3 scant cups; 720 cc) rice
½ burdock root
1 boneless chicken thigh
2 tofu puffs (aburage)
⅓ carrot
½ Tbsp salt
2 Tbsp light soy sauce
⅓ cup sake
2⅔ Tbsp mirin
½ Tbsp sugar
1 snow pea, boiled and julienned, for garnish

**Rinse and slice.**
1. Rinse the rice and let stand in cooker.
2. Shave the gobo into thin strands. Dice the chicken into ⅓ in (1 cm) cubes. Julienne the tofu puffs and the carrot.

**Steam.**

3. Add water to the cooker as usual. Stir in the salt, soy sauce, sake, mirin, and sugar. Level top.

4. Place the chicken, puffs, burdock, and carrot on top (in order) and steam. Stir. Garnish with the snow pea strips.

Slower-cooking and flavor-enhancing ingredients are placed directly on the rice, with others above.

Also Try:
# Vary the ingredients

Oyster Mushrooms, Tofu Puffs, Carrot

Brush and trim 7 oz (200 g) oyster mushrooms. Use with two tofu puffs and ⅓ carrot.

Bamboo Shoots, Chicken, Tofu Puffs, and Carrot

Slice a small cooked bamboo shoot into thin 1 in (2.5 cm). Substitute for the burdock.

# Red Bean Rice

Cool the cooking liquid quickly for brightest color.

Red Bean Rice is served at every festive occasion. Some say the dish is a re-creation of the reddish rice first brought to ancient Japan.

*[5 servings]*
5 rice measures (900 cc) glutinous (mochi) rice
½ cup red cowpeas (sasage)

• The rice-to-cowpea ratio is 10:1.

**Begin a half day ahead.**

1. Rinse the rice, cover with water, and soak for 12 hours.

**Cook the beans.**
2. Place the beans in a pot with plenty of water. Discard any that float. Heat gently so that the water barely shivers, 40 min.
• **Boiling will burst the beans.**

3. Drain, reserving liquid. Fanning with one hand, ladle the liquid with the other to cool the liquid quickly.

**Soak the rice.**

4. When the liquid cools to skin temperature, add the rice and soak 1 hour.

**Steam.**

5. Drain, reserving liquid. Add the beans to the rice and place in a fabric-lined steamer. Leave a space in the center.

6. Boil water in a wok. Place the steamer in the wok and cover. Steam 30 min. on high. Sprinkle some of the reserved bean liquid over the rice. Cover and steam 15 more

To hasten the cooling process, fan the liquid vigorously while scooping and pouring with a ladle. If the liquid cools slowly, the color will fade.

min., sprinkle again, cover again, and steam 15 min. (1 hour total steaming time).

7. Serve with salted black sesame seeds.

35

Seven steps to perfect rice on the stovetop.

## I. Scrub the rice.

1. Place the rice in a pot or a metal basin. Add the water, swirl quickly, and pour off.
•**Round bowls are awkward to press in; plastic is too slippery.**

2. Gather the rice and pull it around (Fig. 1), then press down with your palm (Fig. 2). Continue turning and pressing to scrub off the dirt and particles clinging to the rice.

3. Add more water, swirl, and pour off. (Fig. 3).

4. Repeat steps 2 and 3 three more times (Fig. 4).
•**Scrubbing eliminates the raw flavor and gives a sheen to the cooked rice.**

## II. Rinse.

5. Keep adding more water to the pot (Fig. 5), swirling, and pouring off until the water is clear (Fig. 6).

## III. Drain the rice and let stand.

6. Drain in a strainer and let stand 30 min. to absorb the surface moisture (Fig. 7).
•**Do not soak; it dulls the rice.**

## IV. Add water.

7. Transfer the rice to the pot and add water1 to 2 times the amount of rice (Fig. 8).

## V. Boil.

8. Cover and heat to a boil (Fig. 9). Stir briefly with chopsticks (Fig. 10). Cover and simmer on low, 10 min.

## VI. Steam.

9. When the liquid is absorbed, insert a chopstick at several spots to vent (Fig. 11).
Cover immediately; turn off the heat.

10. Let stand 10 min. on the burner.

## VII. Serve.

11. The rice is now ready to serve. If the grains were scrubbed well, they should now appear polished and shiny (Fig. 12).

12. Stir with a rice paddle, using a cutting motion (Fig. 13).
•**Rice will get sticky if steamed too long.**

13. Transfer to a serving bowl and cover with a well-squeezed wet cloth.
•**Leaving in the pot overcooks the rice.**
•**A wooden rice tub is best for serving.**

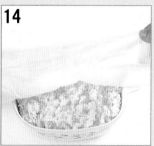

*Key points for rice cookers:
1. If the metal liner is coated, use another metal basin for the scrubbing and rinsing.
2. Let the wet rice stand in a strainer rather than soaking.
3. When ready, transfer to a bowl rather than keeping it warm in the cooker.

Use 1 cup dashi and 1½ Tbsp miso per serving; avoid over-boiling the miso.

## Potato-Tofu Miso

Slow-cooking and flavor-building ingredients go in before the miso.

*[4 servings]*
2 potatoes
1 tofu puff (aburage)
4 cups dashi
6 Tbsp red miso

**Miso goes last.**

1. Quarter the potatoes and slice. Julienne the tofu puff.

2. Add the potatoes to the cold dashi; boil. Add the puff.

3. Dissolve the miso in some hot dashi and stir into the pot.

## Wakame Miso

Delicate, quick-cooking ingredients go in after the miso.

*[4 servings]*
⅒ oz (3 g) dried wakame
½ firm tofu
4 cups dashi
3 Tbsp red miso
3 Tbsp white miso

**Miso goes first.**

1. Soak the wakame as on p. 59. Pull out the thick fiber. Chop. Dice the tofu.

2. Heat the dashi. Dissolve the red and white miso in some hot dashi and add. Stir in the wakame and tofu. Heat. Serve.

## Also Try: More Miso

### Eggplant Miso
*[4 servings]* 1 bunch shimeji mushrooms•
2 Jpnse eggplants•
1 Tbsp oil•4 cups dashi•6 Tbsp red miso

Cut the eggplants into diagonal half rounds and sauté in the oil. Simmer the eggplants and shimeji stalks in the dashi. Add the miso.

### Clam Miso
*[4 servings]* 9 oz (250 g) clams•¼ daikon•4 cups dashi• 6 Tbsp miso

Soak the clams in salted water to expel sand. Julienne the daikon. Simmer the clams and daikon in dashi until the clams open. Add the miso.

### Pumpkin Miso
*[4 servings]* 3½ oz (100 g) kabocha squash•4 thin slices pork•4 cups dashi• 6 Tbsp miso

Dice the squash. Slice the pork to bite size. Heat the squash and pork in dashi until the squash is tender. Add the miso.

*To speed up cooking time for kabocha squash, potatoes, and other dense vegetables, microwave in plastic wrap for 30 sec. first.

*Miso flavor and fragrance varies by region. Combining them results in a rich, complex flavor. Always store miso varieties in separate containers.

For 4 servings, 3 cups dashi and 1 teaspoon salt is standard. For fish or meat soups, add 1 tablespoon sake.

## Hampen Clear Soup

Hampen cooks very quickly.

*[4 servings]*
1 piece hampen (a soft fish cake)
Mitsuba leaves
3 cups dashi
1 tsp salt
1 Tbsp sake

**Season dashi, then simmer.**
1. Slice the hampen into slabs. Chop the mitsuba.
2. Heat the dashi and the salt and sake. Add the hampen and heat briefly. Transfer to bowls and add the mitsuba.

## Egg-Drop Soup

The egg forms beautiful strands in the thickened soup.

*[4 servings]*
2 eggs
2 Tbsp cornstarch
3 cups dashi
1 tsp salt
Green onions for garnish

**Flavor dashi, then thicken it.**
1. Heat the dashi and add the salt. Dissolve the cornstarch in a small dish of water and stir in.

**Add the egg.**
2. Pour the egg into the pot in a thin stream. Do not stir. Turn off the heat when the egg floats up. Garnish; serve.

### Noodles and Egg

[4 servings] 1 bunch somen noodles•4 boiled quail eggs•28 green peas, boiled•3 cups dashi•1 tsp salt

Rubber-band one end of the somen and boil. Plunge in cold water. Arrange ¼ of the somen in each bowl; top with an egg and some peas, add hot, salted dashi.

### White Fish Soup

[4 servings] 1 piece sea bream•cornstarch•3 cups dashi•1 tsp salt•1 Tbsp sake•white part of scallion, julienned
Slice the sea bream, dredge with cornstarch, and blanch. Heat the dashi; add salt and sake. Arrange the sea bream and scallions in bowls. Add dashi.

### Chicken and Myoga

[4 servings] 2 chicken tenderloins•soy sauce•4 myoga (Japanese ginger)•3 cups dashi•1 tsp salt•1 Tbsp sake

Slice the tenderloins and rinse with the soy sauce (p. 46). Julienne the myoga and place in 4 bowls. Simmer the chicken in pre-heated dashi; add the salt and sake.

*Clear soups require a seasonal garnish. Ki no me, young prickly-ash sprigs, are used in the two lefthand soups above but are hard to obtain outside Japan. Other garnishes: scallions, mitsuba, citron peel, sansho powder, black pepper, chili powder.

Dipping sauce for soba; Tokyo-style and Kyoto-style noodle broths.

## Dipping Sauce

*[4 servings]*
2 cups dashi
3 Tbsp mirin
1 Tbsp sugar
½ cup soy sauce

Boil the dashi, mirin, and sugar. Stir in the soy sauce Chill before serving.

## Tokyo-style Broth

*[4 servings]*
5-6 cups dashi
4 Tbsp mirin
2 Tbsp sugar
⅔ cups soy sauce

Boil the dashi, mirin, and sugar. Add the soy sauce; when boiling, serve.

## Kyoto-style Broth

*[4 servings]*
5-6 cups dashi
4 Tbsp mirin
1 Tbsp sugar
½ cup light soy sauce
1 tsp salt

Boil dashi, mirin, and sugar. Add soy sauce and salt. When boiling again, serve.

## Cold Buckwheat Noodles (Zaru Soba)
(Dipping Sauce)

*[1 serving]*
Serve cold boiled buckwheat noodles (soba) with nori, scallions, wasabi, and Dipping Sauce.

## Kitsune Soba
(Tokyo-style Broth)

*[1 serving]*
Rinse cooked buckwheat noodles in boiling water. Serve with Tokyo-style broth, tofu puff (p. 31), kamaboko, kaiware, scallions.

## Kansai Tanuki Udon
(Kyoto-style Broth)

*[1 serving]*
1. Rinse ⅔ of a tofu puff (p. 31). Cut in half, then in strips. Slice diagonally: ½ naganegi (bunching onion), ⅙ narutomaki (spiral-pattern fish cake), 2 snow peas.
2. Heat all with ½ serving of Kyoto-style broth. Thicken with ½ Tbsp cornstarch dissolved in water.
3. Serve with boiled udon noodles and ½ serving of Broth.

## Tokyo Tanuki Udon
*[1 serving]*
Serve boiled udon noodles with: hot Tokyo-style Broth, tempura balls, narutomaki, chopped mitsuba, carrot.

# Chapter 3

# Egg Dishes

Eggs are extremely versatile. They can be hard-boiled, shirred, cooked in savory custards (chawanmushi), or made into tiny sprinkles. Their simple appearance is sometimes deceptive, but these professional tips take away all the guesswork.

*Left to right:* Chicken Custard; Egg Tofu (pp. 46–47).

The proportion of dashi is the main difference between these two dishes.

Custard

⅔ cup dashi for each egg

Egg Tofu

¼ cup dashi for each egg

# Chicken Custard (Chawanmushi) *(photo: p. 44)*

To avoid cracks in the custard, turn the heat low and cook slowly.

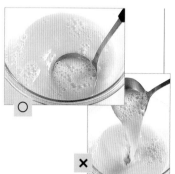

**Season thigh.**

7. Place bowls in a hot steamer. Top with a paper towel. Cover and cook on high 3 min., then on low 10-13 min.
•**Paper catches the water drops.**

*[4 servings]*
3 eggs
2 cups dashi
1 tsp salt
1 tsp light soy sauce
¼ tsp sugar
½ Tbsp sake
3½ oz (100 g) chicken thigh meat
Soy sauce for marinade
Mitsuba (honewort)

3. Stir in the salt, light soy sauce, sugar, and sake.
•**Use the back of a ladle.**

5. Slice the chicken into diagonal pieces. Pour soy sauce over and quickly drain.

**Steam.**

**Prepare the eggs.**
1. Beat the eggs thoroughly without making bubbles.
2. Stir in the dashi with chopsticks, avoiding bubbles.

4. Drape a cloth over a small strainer and gently press the egg mixture through.
•**Do not hold the strainer high.**

6. Divide the chicken among 4 bowls. Gently fill ¾ full with egg mixture.

8. Garnish with chopped mitsuba. Keep covered until serving, so that the custard stays warm.

## Also Try: Seasonal Flavors

**Clams** [Spring]
Use 8-12 sake-steamed clams in place of the chicken. Garnish with kaiware.

**Crab** [Summer]
Use 4 chopped artificial crab sticks and 8 salt-boiled, peeled broad beans.

**Prawns** [Fall]
½ pack shimeji in stalks; 4 peeled sake-steamed prawns; 8 boiled gingko nuts. Mitsuba garnish.

*Note: Ingredients placed on top for illustration only.

## In the Microwave

To prepare in the microwave, use aluminum foil.

1. Follow steps 1-6 at left.
2. Cover tightly with a circle of foil extending halfway down the sides. Prick a hole in the center (figure).
3. Arrange evenly in microwave. To avoid sparks, the foil must not touch the inside walls. Low setting: 4-5 min. for 1; 10-12 min. for 4.

# Egg Tofu
*(photo: page 45)*

Chilled custard with a dab of wasabi is the perfect refresher for a hot summer day.

[For a 2-cup (500-cc) mold]
4 eggs
1¼ cups dashi
⅔ tsp salt
⅔ tsp light soy sauce
⅔ tsp sugar
3 Tbsp sake
Soy-sauce Dashi*
Wasabi (neri-style)
✳ Soy-sauce Dashi: Combine soy sauce and dashi in a 1:1 ratio.

**Combine the ingredients.**
1. Follow steps 1-4 on facing page. The mixture will be slightly thicker.
**Steam.**
2. Gently pour into a square metal mold (nagashi kan) and place in a hot steamer. Steam over high heat 3 min., then 10-13 min. on medium high.

For a smooth surface, strain slowly to prevent bubbles.

The smoothness of the egg tofu is the key to its flavor; pour gently so as not to create bubbles.

3. Place the mold in a basin of cold water.
•**Put chopsticks under the mold so bottom cools quickly, which improves flavor.**

4. Slice into squares. Top with Soy-sauce Dashi, wasabi, and, if available, *ki no ha* (prickly-ash sprigs).

# Thick Omelet

These sweetened omelets are a hit in bento boxes. The sugar content makes them burn easily, so be sure to watch the pan carefully.
Have all the utensils ready before you begin: oiled pan, square of cotton for swabbing, wet dishcloth to cool the pan.

[4 servings]
3 eggs, beaten
2 Tbsp dashi
2 Tbsp sugar
1⅓ Tbsp mirin
2 tsp light soy sauce
Cooking oil

Pour in the raw egg underneath the cooked layer.

**Stir in.**

1. Mix the eggs with the other ingredients.
•**Tilt bowl so sugar will not sink.**

2. Spread a damp dishcloth near stove. Heat a small, oiled pan on medium. Put it on the dishcloth and wait a few sec. until the hissing slows. Return to heat; swab.
•**Cool to prevent egg sticking.**
•**Swab corners and sides too.**

**Cook.**

3. Pour in ¼ of the egg mixture. Prick with chopsticks so that the raw egg seeps under the cooked egg. Detach from sides of pan.

4. With chopsticks, roll omelet from back to front. Push roll to back of pan.

5. Swab with oil and add more egg as in step 3. Lift the roll so egg flows under.

6. Continue as in step 3. Insert chopsticks into the side of the cooked roll and roll up again toward the front. Repeat steps 3–6.

If the egg is not pricked, it will cook unevenly and be difficult to roll.

7. While hot, transfer to board and form into a block with two knives. Slice. Garnish.
•**To form, omelet must be hot.**

More dashi? A soup. Less? A side dish. Either way, these egg dishes satisfy the soul.

# Egg-Drop Mushrooms

The main ingredient is simmered in dashi and then thickened with egg. Try bean sprouts or other crunchy vegetables in this dish.

*[4 servings]*
2 eggs, beaten
1 package enoki mushrooms
1 cup dashi
4 Tbsp mirin
2 Tbsp light soy sauce

**Chop.**
1. Trim the roots from the enoki mushrooms. Separate into stalks.

**Simmer.**
2. Bring the dashi and mirin to a boil. Add the soy sauce and the enoki.

3. When heated through, pour egg into openings made by chopsticks.

4. Cover and steam on low until eggs just begin to firm. Serve in bowls.

# Egg-Drop Myoga

This soup-like dish works best with fragrant vegetables. Try with udo, leeks, or fennel.

*[4 servings]*
2 eggs
6 myoga (Japanese ginger)
2 cups dashi
1 Tbsp mirin
½ tsp salt

**Slice.**

1. Slice the myoga in half lengthwise, then julienne.

**Simmer.**

2. Boil the dashi and mirin. Add the salt and myoga.

3. Heat through, then add the egg in a thin stream. Fluff the egg with chopsticks. Serve.

From left: Egg-Drop Mushrooms; Egg-Drop Myoga bulk.

## Boiled Eggs

Pierce a tiny hole to prevent cracks and keep the yolk in the center.

1. Using an awl or an ice pick, pierce a tiny hole in the round end (Fig. 1). The round end contains an air chamber. The hole allows air to escape without cracking the shell.

2. Place the eggs in a bowl and add warm water. The air will bubble out (Fig. 2).

3. When the bubbles stop, gently lower eggs into boiling water. Boil gently for 6–11 min. Plunge in ice water. *After 11 min., the surface of the yolk will turn grey.

## Hot Spring Eggs

Make Japanese-style shirred eggs just with 3 changes of water.

1. Follow steps 1 and 2 at left.

2. When the bubbles stop, drain. Add boiling water to the bowl (Figure). Let cool to skin temperature. Drain and repeat twice.

3. While the eggs are cooking, bring 1/3 cup dashi and 1/3 cup soy sauce to a boil with 1 1/2 Tbsp mirin. Cool. Crack the eggs into a serving bowl. Serve with the dashi mixture and wasabi.

▼6 minutes
Yolk totally
liquid

8 minutes ▶
Yolk has
liquid center

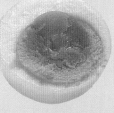

9 minutes ▶
Yolk softly
cooked

11 minutes ▶
Firm yolk

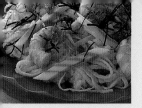

## Golden Threads

Cornstarch lends a sheen and texture to the egg strands.

3 eggs
2 Tbsp sugar
Pinch salt
½ tsp cornstarch
Cooking oil

1. Beat the eggs well with the sugar and salt. Dissolve the cornstarch in water and stir in (Fig. 1).

2. Strain the egg mixture through cotton fabric in a sieve.

3. Heat a small pan on low. Cool briefly on a damp towel, then return to heat and spread with oil, using a bit of fabric.

4. Ladle some of the egg into the pan. Tilt to coat (Fig. 2).

5. Move the pan in circles above the burner. When almost dry, invert omelet (Fig. 3) and cook 3-5 sec.

6. Repeat steps 3-5 with remaining egg. Stack and cut into two, then fold and julienne (Fig 4).

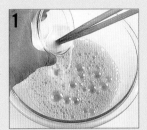
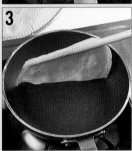

## Egg Sprinkles

Keep the heat high. Use a damp towel to control the temperature.

3 eggs
2 Tbsp sugar
Pinch salt

1. Beat the egg, sugar, and salt in a small pan (Fig. 1).

2. Fasten 6 chopsticks with a rubber band (Fig. 2).

3. Heat the egg pan on medium, stirring with the chopsticks (Fig. 3). Cool the pan on a damp towel when clumps form.
·**High heat cooks the egg through.**

4. Return to heat and continue stirring until mostly cooked. Return to the towel.

5. Return to heat. When moist, remove from heat and continue stirring.

6. Press through a strainer.

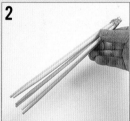

# Chapter 4

# Beans and Dried Foods

## Tastes of Home

Sweet, long–simmered beans, crumbly tofu lees stewed with vegetables—these homey preparations are rarely offered at Japanese restaurants because chefs dare not compete with anyone's cherished family recipe. Now you can bring these slow-cooked treasures to your table and begin your own family tradition.

*Left to right:* Five Treasure Beans; Simmered Kidney Beans (pp. 56–57).

# Five Treasure Beans *(photo: p. 54)*

Soak the beans thoroughly for faster cooking.

The other ingredients add texture and color to the protein-rich beans. Boil off the liquid completely to help this delicious dish keep well.

**Cook the beans.**

2. Pour the beans into a pot with enough soaking water to cover well.

3. Bring to a boil on medium. Skim the foam. In water just hot enough for the beans to dance, cook 40-50 min. Add water as needed.

**Cut to size.**

4. Boil the konnyaku from cold water. Cut it and the carrots and jellyfish into ⅓ in (1 cm) dice.

**Add to the pot.**

5. Stir the dice in.

6. Simmer 10 min., till carrots are soft. Mix sugar, mirin, and soy sauce. Add. Rinse bowl with some bean mixture.

Since the beans will cook in their soaking liquid, they need to be rinsed first. Soak 8–12 hours in plenty of water.

7. Continue cooking 20 min., until liquid evaporates.

[ *4 servings* ]
1 cup dried soybeans
½ piece konnyaku (devil's-tongue jelly)
⅓ carrot
¾ oz (20 g) dried jellyfish
½ cup sugar
½ cup mirin
½ cup soy sauce

*The sugar, mirin, and soy sauce are in a 1:1:1 ratio.

**Soak the beans.**
1. Rinse the beans in cold water. Soak overnight in plenty of water.

56

# Simmered Kidney Beans *(photo: p. 55)*

(photo: p. 55)

For best color, boil beans in their soaking water.

Some dishes are not finished when the cooking stops. In this one, the sugar and soy sauce do not quite harmonize when the dish is still hot. But as it cools, the flavors meld beautifully with the beans.

*[4 servings]*
1 cup kidney beans
1½ cups sugar
3 Tbsp soy sauce

**Soak the beans.**
1. Rinse the beans and soak in plenty of water for 8-12 hours.

**Cook the beans.**

2. Pour the beans into a pot with enough soaking water to cover well.

3. Boil. Skim off the foam. In water just hot enough for the beans to dance, cook 50 min.

4. Cook until you can crush one with your fingers.
•**Avoid burns!**

**Add flavorings.**

5. Stir in the sugar. Skim the foam. Lower the heat and simmer 20 min.

Do not discard the soaking water, it lends both color and flavor to the beans.

6. When the beans are shiny, add the soy sauce. Simmer 5 min., just until the soy odor has cooked off. Let stand to cool.

# Soaking times, bulk increases, and cooking times for 16 dried goods

**Soybeans** Soak 8–12 hours (2–2.5x); cook 40–50 min.

**Toramame** Soak 8–12 hours (2–2.5x); cook 40–50 min.

**Kidney beans** Soak 8–12 hours (2.5–3x); cook 50 min.

**Green soybeans** Soak 8–12 hours (2–2.5x); cook 40–50 min.

**Large white kidney beans (shiro hana mame)** Soak 8–12 hours (1.5–2x); cook 50–60 min.

**Red cowpeas (sasage)** No soaking needed; cook 40 min. (3x).

**Large black beans (murasaki hana mame)** Soak overnight (1.5–2x); cook 50–60 min.

**Great Northern beans** Soak 8–12 hours (1.5–2x); cook 60 min.

**Azuki beans** No soaking needed; cook 30–40 min. (3x).

NOTE: The x represents the volume increase. 2x = double in bulk.

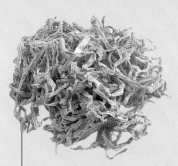

**Shredded Daikon** Soak as on p. 63 for 10–15 min. (2x).

**Freeze–Dried Tofu** Soak as on p. 64. Soaking time varies.

**Hijiki** (edible brown algae) Soak as on p. 65 for 30–40 min. (3x).

**Kampyo** (dried gourd strips) Soak as on p. 67 for 5–10 min. (width 2x).

**Dried Shiitake** Cover with water. Float a plate on top (Figure). Soak 40–60 min. (2x).
*The soaking water can be used as stock.

**Dried Wakame** Soften 2–3 min. in water (3x). Remove the spine and chop. Add hot water (Figure), then plunge in cold water.

**Fu** (Wheat–gluten rings) Soak 40–50 min as on p. 69 (2–3x).

NOTE: Dried goods should be nearly used up in time for the next new crop. Store in a cool, dry place to avoid mold and pests.

# White Beans and Chicken

Stir gently to avoid crushing the soft beans, and dissolve the miso before adding.

Plump beans and tender chicken simmered in a miso base. Even young people who dislike beans will enjoy this dish.

*[4 servings]*
1 cup Great Northern or other white beans
1 chicken thigh
½ Tbsp sugar
1½ Tbsp white miso
1½ Tbsp soy sauce
5-6 snow peas, boiled in salted water

•The sugar, miso, and soy sauce are in a 1:3:3 ratio.

**Soak and boil the beans.**
1. Following steps 1-4 on page 57, soak the beans 8-12 hours and cook 50-60 min. on medium.

**Add the chicken.**

2. Trim the fat and cut into bite-sized pieces. When the beans are tender, stir in the chicken and raise the heat to high. Skim off the foam and any fat.

3. When the chicken is cooked through, add the sugar. Dissolve the miso as at far right, then add.

4. Stir in the soy sauce in a big circle with the thick ends of the chopsticks.
•**Use thick ends for fragile foods.**

5. Continue cooking undisturbed until the liquid is almost gone. Tilt the pot and flip the contents (see p. 15). Garnish with snow peas.

These beans are so soft that they easily disintegrate when stirred. To avoid bruising the beans, dissolve the miso in some of the cooking liquid before adding to the pot.

# Dried Daikon and Tofu Puffs

Dried daikon strips are rich in calcium and fiber, quick to soak, and easy to work with. If unavailable, try asking for Thai dried turnip (hor chai bo), sold in some Asian markets.

*[4 servings]*
2½ oz (70 g) dried daikon strips
1 aburage (deep-fried tofu)
¾ oz (20 g) carrots
2 cups dashi
4 Tbsp sugar
⅓ cup mirin
⅓ cup soy sauce

**Soak and chop the daikon**
1. Soak, knead, and chop the daikon as shown at far right.

**Slice other items**
2. Rinse the aburage (p. 31) and cut strips ⅓ in (1 cm) wide. Cut carrot into 1 in (4 cm) matchsticks.

**Simmer.**
3. Boil the dashi, mirin, and sugar. Add the soy sauce.

4. Add the aburage.
·**Add stock-flavoring items first.**

5. Add daikon and simmer 10 min.

6. Add carrots and cook till just tender.

Knead the daikon strips in water (Fig. 1). The water will become cloudy and the dried-goods smell will vanish. Soak 10–15 min., then squeeze well to avoid over-softening. Chop at several points (Fig. 2), then turn the board and chop once more (Fig. 3) so that no stray long pieces remain.

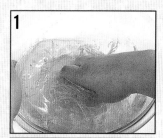

# Simmered Tofu

Freeze-dried tofu responds differently by supplier: check the label.

Freeze-dried tofu is available in specialty markets.

[4 servings]
3 cups dashi
2 Tbsp sugar
⅓ cup mirin
⅓ cup light soy sauce
Citron zest

**Soak the tofu.**
1. If the freeze-dried tofu requires soaking (check the label), follow the steps at right.

**Simmer.**
2. Combine the dashi, sugar, and mirin in a pot and boil. Add the soy sauce, then the tofu.

3. Cover with wet circle of rice paper. Simmer 15-20 min.

4. Slice and serve with the citron zest.

Until recently, freeze-dried tofu had to be rinsed many times because ammonia was used in processing. Today, most types require only a short soak; others crumble if soaked at all. For the soaking type, use water at the specified temperature. Squeeze the tofu between your palms (Fig. 1). For the non-soaking type, simply place the tofu directly in the simmering liquid (Fig. 2).

# Seafood Salad

Sand from the hijiki sinks to the bottom; lift gently.

A light and fresh salad made from hijiki and other seafood.

*[4 servings]*
¾ oz (20 g) hijiki (edible brown algae)
¼ head cabbage
½ piece kamaboko (fish cake)
½ cup mayonnaise
2 Tbsp umeboshi, pitted
Salt for boiling

**Soak and boil.**

1. Soak the hijiki as at right. Boil until soft, then rinse in cold water and drain.

**Combine.**
2. Chop the cabbage and boil in salted water. Drain and plunge in cold water. Squeeze well. Slice the kamaboko into ¼ in (5 mm) strips.
3. Combine the mayonnaise and umeboshi. Toss with the other ingredients.

Soak the hijiki thoroughly for 30–40 min. in plenty of water. Sand will have settled to the bottom. Gently lift the hijiki out of the bowl and place in a strainer (Fig. 1). Lower the strainer into a bowl of fresh water (Fig. 2) and shake out any additional sand.

# Miso-Dressed Gourd Strips

Kampyo, usually in a supporting role, gets to be the star in this dish. Use thick strips for best texture.

[4 servings]
½ soft (momen) tofu
⅔ tsp miso
1½ Tbsp roasted sesame seeds
3 Tbsp sugar
½ Tbsp light soy sauce
½ Tbsp mirin
Pinch salt
¾ oz (25 g) kampyo (dried gourd strips)
1 cup dashi
½ Tbsp light soy sauce
2 Tbsp mirin
5 snow peas, julienned on the diagonal
Salt

**Miso dressing.**
1. Follow steps 1-6 on pp. 112-113.

**Simmer.**

2. Prepare kampyo as at right and chop. Boil the dashi, soy sauce, and mirin; add kampyo. Stir gently for 10 min. Cool in the liquid. Drain and squeeze gently.

**Blanch.**
3. Blanch the snow peas in salted water. Drain. Fan to cool.

**Combine.**

4. Add the kampyo to the dressing. Add the snow peas.

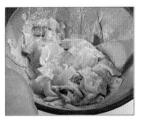

5. Stir with a wooden rice paddle.
•**Avoids breakage.**

Rub with salt to remove the dried-goods taste.

Rinse the kampyo. Sprinkle with 1 tsp salt and rub well (Fig. 1) to soften the kampyo and remove the dried-goods taste.

Rinse off the salt. Soak in plenty of fresh water (Fig 2) for 5-10 min.

Boil the kampyo in its soaking water (Fig. 3) for about 10 min., until translucent (Fig 4). Drain, rinse, and squeeze well.

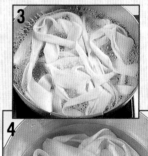

# Okinawa-style Fu and Eggs

Okinawa-style fu (wheat-gluten rings) is softer than the standard style. This egg sauté gives it an almost syrupy texture. If Okinawa-style fu is not available, any style of fu will serve nicely.

*[4 servings]*
3 oz (80 g) fu (wheat-gluten rings)
3 eggs
1½ cups dashi
¼ cups light soy sauce
2 Tbsp mirin
3 Tbsp cooking oil
Spinach
Salt

**Soak the fu.**
1. Reconstitute the fu as shown at right.

**Sauté.**

2. Sauté the fu in the oil on medium high. Do not let them burn. Add the dashi and simmer; add the soy sauce and mirin. Stir occasionally with a wooden spoon.

**Add the egg.**

3. When the liquid has almost been absorbed, swirl in the egg and cook until nearly set. Garnish with blanched spinach.

Place the fu in a bowl with plenty of water. Submerge each piece in the water by hand (Fig. 1).

Let stand 40–50 min. until soft (Fig. 2) but not waterlogged. (If soaked too long, they will fall apart when cooked.)

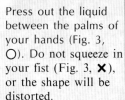
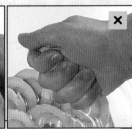

Press out the liquid between the palms of your hands (Fig. 3, ○). Do not squeeze in your fist (Fig. 3, ✗), or the shape will be distorted.

# Vegetable Medley

Tofu lees (okara) are available where fresh tofu is made.

Strained tofu lees have a delicious texture.

**[4 servings]**
14 oz (400 g) tofu lees (okara)
½ chicken thigh
½ gobo (burdock root)
⅓ carrot
½ konnyaku (devil's tongue jelly)
3 fresh shiitake
1 oz (30 g) dried tree-ear fungus, soaked
2 cups dashi
½ cup mirin
½ cup sugar
½ cup light soy sauce
1 scallion (green part)

•Dashi, mirin, sugar, soy sauce ratio:
4:1:1:1.

**Prepare okara.**
1. Prepare okara as at right.

**Chop.**

2. Trim fat from the chicken and dice. Boil chopped gobo until tender. Cut the carrot into 1 in (3 cm) julienne. Boil konnyaku and dice. Dice the shiitake and tree ear. Chop the scallion.

**Simmer.**
3. Boil dashi, mirin, and sugar in a large pot. Add soy sauce. Add all from step 2 except scallion and carrot. Remove foam.

4. Add the carrot and crumble in the tofu lees. Stirring with a wooden paddle, cook on medium high for 10 min. (burns easily). When almost dry, add the scallion and serve.

With a ladle, push the okara through a strainer (a silk sieve if available) in a bowl of water (Fig. 1).

The okara will sink into the water (Fig. 2), leaving the soy casings in the strainer.

Discard the casings. Line the strainer with fabric and pour the okara water through it (Fig 3). Drain.

Squeeze out the water through the fabric (Fig. 4). The fine, white okara is ready for use.

Strained okara          Leftover soy casings

# Chapter 5

# Seafood Cooking

Since ancient times, seafood has been one of the most important elements of Japanese cooking. Every technique from slicing to serving has been perfected over centuries. Let's explore these time–honored methods in detail.

*Left to right:* Flounder Rolls; Tuna and Squid Sashimi　　　　　　　　　(pp. 74–75)

Professional secrets for slicing and serving beautifully.

## Pull Cut

Pull the knife toward you as you slice. Use for rectangles, cubes, and julienne.

**From the right, slice with one pull.**

1. Lay the sashimi flat. Starting from the right edge, rest the base of the knife on the fish (Fig. 1) and pull back and down with one motion (Fig. 2). •Slice ¼ in (8–9 mm) thick; thinner for fatty cuts.

2. After slicing, layer each piece on the right side of the board.

## Slanted Cut

This softer slice is used for dense sashimi or the thin flesh toward the tail.

**From the left, slice with a tilted blade.**
1. Lay the sashimi close to you. Slant the blade and slice ⅛ in (2–3 mm) thick. .

2. Flip each piece and layer at the top of the board.
•The underside has clean edges.

## Serving

A single serving is the best place to start. Large platters follow the same method.

**Garnish (tsuma).**
1. Mound the garnish at the back toward the left.
•Try julienned daikon or onion.

2. Fold back the bottom of a shiso leaf and place it at an angle.
•The folding symbolizes care "to the hem."

•The leaf shields the sashimi from the garnish.

**Place the sashimi.**
3. Layer the sashimi so it falls back to the right.
•A right-handed person can easily pick up one piece at a time.

**Add a vegetable.**
4. Place a bright, complementary vegetable such as bitter melon, cucumber, or green onions.

**Ginger or wasabi**
5. Place a hill of ginger or wasabi to the right.

# Tuna and Squid Sashimi
*(photo: p. 73)*

*[4 servings]*
2 pieces tuna (maguro)•1 piece squid (mongo ika) for sashimi•julienned daikon*• 1 shiso leaf•grated wasabi

1. Slant-cut the squid and pull-cut the tuna (Fig. 1).
2. Mound the daikon at the back and spread with a leaf of shiso. Place the tuna on a diagonal. The top row (if any) goes to the left of the bottom row.
3. Spread another shiso on the right. Place the squid on it (Fig. 2). Place a hill of wasabi in front.
**•The flow goes from the back left to the front right.**
∗Slice a 3 in (9 cm) piece of daikon into a thin strip as if peeling it. Slice into threads.

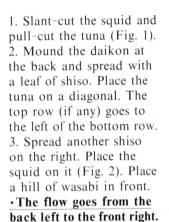

# Seared Bonito

*[4 servings]*
1. Pull-slice the seared bonito.
2. Thinly slice an onion and soak. Seed and slice 1 in (4 cm) bitter melon and blanch.
3. Serve as shown, with shiso leaf and grated ginger.

# Flounder Rolls *(photo: p. 72)*

*[4 servings]* 10½ oz (300 g) flounder•5 shiso leaves•2-3 umeboshi

1. Slant-cut the flounder into ⅛ in slices.
2. Seed and crush the umeboshi.
3. Dab a bit of umeboshi on one piece of flounder. Roll up and encircle with a strip of shiso.

# Miso Mackerel

# The salt prep for the mackerel is the key.

Autumn is the season for mackerel. The fat melts into the miso. We use red miso here, but you can use your favorite variety.

*[4 servings]*
1 mackerel
Salt
2 cups water
⅓ cup mirin
⅓ cup sugar
⅓ cup soy sauce
2 Tbsp red miso
Ginger

•The water, mirin, sugar, soy sauce ratio is 6:1:1:1.

**Marinate.**
1. Remove the head and cut into 4 pieces. Rinse the cavity.

2. Salt the skin. For a fatty autumn fish, let stand 30-40 min. Leaner fish need 15 min.

3. When the surface has sweated, the salt is almost invisible, and the skin looks stretched, rinse.

**Simmer.**

4. Boil the water, mirin, and sugar. Add soy sauce. At the boil, add the mackerel. Top with a paper lid (p. 21). Simmer 15-20 min.

5. Uncover. Stir some liquid into the miso. Ladle the miso over the mackerel, then the liquid over the miso. Cook a few min. more.
•**Do not stir.**

The salt draws out the fluid in the fat layer and firms it. It also keeps the skin from separating during the cooking.

6. Julienne the ginger along the grain. Rinse in water. Mound the ginger on the mackerel to serve.

# Simmered Turbot

Turbot with its eggs (komochi karei) is widely available in Japan (fresh and frozen) but more difficult to find elsewhere. Turbot without eggs works just as well.

[ *4 servings* ]
4 pieces turbot
2 cups water
1/3 cup mirin
1/2 cup sugar
1/2 cup soy sauce
Fresh ginger

• Water, mirin, sugar, and soy sauce are in a 6:2:3:3 ratio.

**Scale the fish.**

1. Scrape off any scales with the tip of the knife.

Cook the turbot in a single layer to prevent breakage.

Turning or moving the fish in the pot will make it fall apart. Also, add the turbot after the sauce is boiling, to avoid a raw flavor.

**Simmer.**
2. Boil water, mirin, and sugar. Add the soy sauce. At the boil, add the turbot and boil again.

3. Cover with paper lid (p. 15) and cook 20 min. on low.

4. Garnish with ginger (p. 77).

Also Try: # Cooking with Bony Parts

**Fins and Tails**

1. Rinse bony fragments (flounder is used here). Sprinkle with salt (Fig. 1; more for fatty fish) and let stand 30 min. to sweat.
2. Pour hot water to firm the flesh (Fig. 2; removes raw flavor) and plunge in ice water.
3. Remove any scales or innards (Fig 3). Drain in a colander.
4. Simmer as for Simmered Turbot. Garnish with boiled snow peas.

Salt-Grilled Horse Mackerel (Aji), p. 83

Salt-Grilled Sweetfish (Ayu), p. 83

Yellowtail Teriyaki, p. 83

Simple salt-grilled fish becomes even more delicious when these steps are followed.

## 1. Clean the fish.

For fish that has not been cleaned:

•**Scales** Scrape the fish with the back of a cleaver.

•**Innards** Make a slit in the belly and remove the innards (upper fig.).

•**Gills** Lift flap and detach gills at top and bottom (lower fig.). Remove. Repeat on other side.

•**Blood** Rinse the cavities. Pat dry.

## 2. Make Slits.

For ocean fish, a slit on the back speeds cooking. River fish do not need the slit.

•**Back Slit** Make a deep incision along the back (upper fig.).
•**X Slit** Cut an X into the left side (lower fig.).

## 3. Skewer.

Techniques suggest the rippling of ocean waves or the effort of swimming upstream.

•**Rippled** (ocean fish). Insert in soft spot behind right cheek *(right)*. Turn just past left gills. Pierce right center and turn again. Stop at ¾ point, then turn again to exit on right.

•**Upstream** (river fish). Start behind the left eye. Pierce the right side. Turn and push to the ⅔ point. Turn and exit near the tail.

•**Second skewer.** Steadies the fish for the rack. Start at the head, crossing the first skewer. Push out near the tail.

## 4. Salt.

To serve hot, salt just before grilling. To serve cold, salt in advance.

•**Fin salt.** Salt the fins and tail well to prevent burns *(top)*.

•**Drop salt.** Sprinkle evenly from about 12 in (30 cm) above *(bottom)*.

## 5. Grill.

Start grilling on the left side, or the side that will be on top when served.

•**Heat Below** (toasting net) Left side down: medium high. Twist the skewer occasionally for easy removal. When golden, turn over and cook till done.

•**Heat Above** (broiler *middle*) or Heat on Both Sides (fish cooker, *bottom*). Skewering not needed. Under a broiler, turn over halfway through the cooking.

## Salt-Grilled Horse Mackerel *(photo: p. 80)*

*[4 servings]* 4 horse mackerel•salt• Myoga (p. 91)

1. Clean the fish. Shave off the thin row of center scales from the tail. Make a back slit and an X slit.
2. Ripple skewer; second skewer.
3. Fin salt and drop salt. Grill.
4. Serve on bamboo leaves with sliced myoga.

## Salt-Grilled Sweetfish *(photo: p. 80)*

*[4 servings]* 4 sweetfish•salt•tade-su

1. Grasping both eyes, rinse, then scrape scales with tip of blade. Do not remove gills/innards.
2. Upstream skewer; second skewer.
3. Fin salt and drop salt. Grill.
4. Serve with tade (knotweed) and tade-su (tade-su made with knotweed)

## Yellowtail Teriyaki *(photo: p. 81)*

*[4 servings]* 4 pieces yellowtail•Grilling Sauce (p. 103)•Plum Wine Lotus Root (p. 91)

1. Coat well with the sauce and let stand 30-60 min.
2. Cook from the top side first. Turn.
3. Garnish with the lotus root.

For pan-fried teriyaki, add the sauce at the end.

The sauce burns easily in the hot pan, so it is added at the end. Also, salmon does not need to be marinated.

# Salmon Teriyaki

Use a frying pan for quick and simple teriyaki.

[*4 servings*]
4 pieces fresh salmon
Pastry flour
2 Tbsp Grilling Sauce
(p. 103)
1 Tbsp cooking oil
Sweet chestnuts

**Dredge salmon.**

1. Dredge the salmon in the flour, shaking off the excess.

**Fry.**

2. Heat the oil in a pan. Place the salmon face down. Cook 2–3 min., then turn and cook 2–3 min. more. Do not overcook.

·**The top side cooks first while the pan is clean.**

3. Lower the heat and add the sauce. Remove from heat. Coat in the sauce. Serve with chestnut.

Seal the foil well to hold in the steam.

Fold into a triangle. Fold over the open sides. Roll and fold around the edges to form a half circle.

# White Fish in Foil

Serve with buttered soy sauce or soy sauce and lemon.

[4 servings]
4 pieces white fish
1 pkg shimeji mushrooms
1 pkg enoki mushrooms
Spinach
Sake
Salt

**Prepare all.**
1. Slit the flesh along the small back bones and pull them out. Repeat with the bones near the bottom of the tail.

2. Marinate 30 min. in salted sake.

3. Separate the shimeji and enoki.

**Wrap and cook.**

4. Place fish and mushrooms on a square of foil. Wrap as shown (top right).

5. Cook the packets in a pan on medium low 10 min. until the foil expands. Open. Garnish with steamed spinach.

# Simmered Squid

Start the cooking in cold water for tender flavor.

Squid and octopus are tender when first cooked, then become tough, and then, after a long simmer, become tender again.

4 cuttlefish (surume ika)
1 pkg ito konnyaku (devil's-tongue jelly noodles)
5 cups water
¾ cups sugar
¾ cups mirin
⅔ cups soy sauce
Broad beans (fava)
Salt

**Prepare cuttlefish.**

1. Remove the legs and rinse the cavity. Cut a vent in the top of the cavity.

2. Cut the legs off below the eyes. Remove the mouth. Trim off the tough tips of the legs.

**Stuff the cavity.**
3. Put the konnyaku in cold water and boil. Use full length.

4. Fill cavities with legs and konnyaku. Seal with toothpicks.

**Simmer.**
5. Mix water, soy sauce, sugar, mirin.

6. Add squid. Heat to boil. Remove foam. Cover with a wet rice paper lid and cook 80 min. on low.

For fish, the liquid must be boiling first. Cuttlefish, squid, and octopus cook best when started in cold liquid.

7. Slice into rounds. Boil the beans in salted water and use for garnish.

# Simmered Scallops

1. For untrimmed scallops, pull back the skirt and remove the greyish sac. It has a sandy texture and may contain harmful bacteria.

**Simmer.**
2. Boil the water, sugar, and mirin. Add the soy sauce.

3. At the second boil, add scallops. When boiling and scallops are puffed (2–3 min.), remove.

4. Boil until sauce starts to thicken and the bubbles are smaller (2 min.).

5. Add the scallops. Cook 1–2 min. until scallops show above sauce level. Remove.

6. Boil sauce another 2–3 min. until fully bubbling as shown. Reduce heat.

Simmer and remove, simmer and remove: This repetition is the key for tenderness. The process is simpler than it looks: it only takes 15 min.

[4 servings]
10½ oz (300 g) scallops
1 cup water
2 Tbsp sugar
¼ cup mirin
¼ cup soy sauce
Roasted sesame seeds

Over continuous high heat, boil and remove twice for tender scallops.

Scallops toughen easily even over low heat. Brief cooking on high is the trick.

7. Continue simmering until thick. Add the scallops. Stir to coat. Remove from heat.

8. Serve with sesame seeds.

# Steamed Clams

This dish is so simple that there are no special tricks. The juices of the clams blend with the sake for an intense flavor.

[4 servings]
26 oz (700 g) short-necked clams (asari)
3 Tbsp sake
½ tsp salt
Mitsuba or cilantro

**Soak the clams**.
1. To expel sand, soak for 30 min. in a cool dark place in almost enough 2% salt water (sea water) to cover. Rinse.
**Steam**.
2. Heat clams, sake, and salt on medium. Cover. When clams begin to open, uncover. Stir gently until all are open. Add chopped mitsuba or cilantro and serve.

Clams overcook easily—serve as soon as the shells open.

To cook evenly, shake the pot occasionally and uncover if it is about to boil over.

Mackerel, one of the simplest fishes to work with, is used in these photographs.

## Rounds

For simmered dishes such as Miso Mackerel (p. 76). Even the most delicate flesh will not fall apart.

1. Cut off the head just below the gills (Fig. 1).

2. Pull out innards (Fig. 2). Rinse, scraping with chopstick (Fig. 3). Pat dry.

3. Cut off the tail. Slice into rounds (4 pieces for mackerel; fig. 4).

## Mackerel Fillets

Step1-4 are for two -piece filleting; steps 1-6 are for boneless fillets (p. 101)

1. With one stroke, cut off the head below the side fin (Fig. 1).

2. Make an incision through the belly (Fig. 2). Scrape out the innards. Rinse well. Thoroughly pat dry.

3. Insert the knife into the cut end just above the bone (Fig. 3). Slice across.
·**Soft mackerel requires this one-cut method.**

4. Bone-in filleting (nimai-oroshi, or two-piece slicing) is complete (Fig. 5).

5. Insert the blade just above the center of the bone-in fillet (Fig. 6). Slice along the center bone (Fig 7).

6. Two boneless fillets are now complete (Fig. 8: sanmai-oroshi, or three-piece slicing).

### Removing the stomach bones

Insert the knife just below the stomach bones. Pressing the bones gently, slice out the bones.

### Pulling out the side bones

Running your finger along the center, pull out the small bones with kitchen tweezers. The angle of the pull should match the angle of the bone.

# Boneless Filleting for Other Fish

For fish other than mackerel, slice in from the back and belly rather than straight across.

1. Follow mackerel steps 1 and 2. From the back (Fig. 1), cut along the backbone down to the center.

2. Turn the fish around and cut along the ribs from the belly to the center (Fig. 2).

3. Insert the knife just above the thick center bone. Slice slowly down through the side of the tail.

4. Repeat on the other side (Fig. 4).
•**Move the knife bit by bit for a clean cut.**

**Sweet Marinated Myoga** (photo: p. 83)
Boil myoga for 30-60 sec. Drain. Blanket with salt and let stand 10-15 min. Rinse. Marinate 5 min. in 1:1 water:vinegar.

**Plum Wine Lotus Root** (photo: p. 83)
Boil sliced lotus root in vinegared water. Rinse. Marinate in plum wine 1 day.

# Chapter 6

# Pan-Fried and
## Deep-Fried Dishes

Fried foods are rare in Japanese cuisine. Perhaps this is why tempura and the other dishes in this chapter are so popular in Japan and abroad. It takes practice to find the perfect temperature, but the results are well worth it.

Tempura (pp. 94–95)

# Tempura *(photo: p. 93)*

The fluffy coating on restaurant tempura is hard to mimic at home but not impossible. First goal: eliminate sogginess.

[4 servings]
1 egg
⅔ cup water
1 cup pastry flour
2 Tbsp sake*
4 prawns
8 Japanese peppers or 2 green bell peppers
2 Japanese eggplants
4 sillago or smelt, butterflied
4 diagonal slices yams, ⅓ in (1 cm) thick
4 slices kabocha squash, ⅓ in (1 cm) thick
4 asparagus
More pastry flour
1½ cups dashi
3 Tbsp soy sauce or more
4 Tbsp mirin
Grated daikon
Grated ginger
Cooking oil

*The sake cleanses the flavor of meat and seafood. Not needed for vegetable-only tempura.

**Make the batter.**

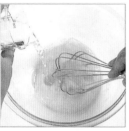

1. Beat the egg with a wire whisk, lifting up, without making bubbles. Add the water and sake.
•**Use a large bowl. In a small bowl, the flour gets overmixed.**

2. Add the flour.

3. Whisk gently in a figure-8 pattern. Lumps should remain.
•**Whisk immediately or the flour will clump. Avoid overmixing.**

4. Chill until ready for use.
•**Cold batter fries up light.**

**Trim the prawns.**
5. Push out the vein with a bamboo skewer.

6. Peel, leaving tail on. Scrape out the water from the tail. Bend the sharp tip.

7. Make shallow incisions in the belly at ⅓ in (1 cm) intervals. Bend back and devein.

### Slice.

8. Slice remaining ingredients as shown.

Japanese peppers. Trim the stem. Make a small slit to prevent bursting.

Bell pepper. Cut in half lengthwise. Cut out the core but leave the ridges.
· **Do not trim off ridges or pepper will split.**

Eggplant. Trim stem. Slice in half or half rounds. Slash to speed cooking.

Sillago or smelt. Ask for tempura-ready butterflied fish.

Slice the yam and kabocha ⅓ in (1 cm) thick. Trim the asparagus.

### Fry the seafood.

9. Fill ¾ of the pot with oil and heat.
· **Choose a thick, deep pan to keep the heat high.**

10. At 360°F (180°C), dip the prawns and fish in pastry flour and then in the batter. Fry. Do not crowd (60% of surface). Turn to cook evenly. When pale gold and fluffy, remove and drain.
· **Dust seafood with flour under the batter, to avoid sogginess.**

### Vegetables next.

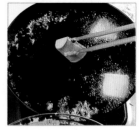

11. Batter the vegetables. Fry peppers, eggplant, and asparagus at 360°F (180°C).

12. Lower the heat for pumpkin and yams, for best aroma. Test for doneness with a bamboo skewer.

13. Boil the dashi, soy sauce, and mirin. Serve tempura on paper, with the dipping sauce and condiments.

# Pork and Onion Fritters

Break up thick spots with chopsticks.

Ordinary ingredients become extraordinary when combined in these light fritters.

*[4 servings]*
1 large egg
⅔ cup water
1¼ cups pastry flour
2 Tbsp sake
1 onion
3 oz (80 g) thinly sliced pork, bite size

**Slice.**
1. Slice the onion very thin.

**Make the batter.**
2. Follow steps 1–4 on p. 94. Slightly more flour is used for fritters.

**Fry.**

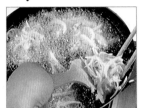

3. Coat the onion

and pork in batter. With a rice paddle, slide a cluster into 350–360°F (170–180° C) oil.

**·If cluster does not spread out a bit, thin the batter. If it scatters, lower heat.**

4. Turn over. Loosen any clumps.

5. Remove when fluffy and light.

*Serve with sweet-pepper tempura and soy sauce.

For light and tasty fritters, use just enough batter to hold the ingredients together. Use chopsticks to loosen any thick clumps—prevents raw spots.

## Also Try: More Combinations

**Shrimp and Mitsuba**
Peel, devein, and chop 3½ oz (100 g) shrimp. Cut mitsuba to 1 in (3 cm) lengths.

**Carrots and Gobo**
Julienne 2 oz (60 g) each of carrots and gobo (burdock root).

**Squid and Onion**
Pound the legs of 2 squid (prevents splattering) and chop. Thinly slice 1 small onion.

**Scallops and Bamboo Shoots** Slice 3½ oz (100 g) scallops to bite size and dredge in flour. Slice 3½ oz (100 g) cooked bamboo shoots.

**Dried Shrimp and Onion**
Thinly slice 1 small onion. Chop Mitsuba. Use 1-3/4 oz (50 g) dried shrimp.

# Fried Tofu in Broth

Seasonal garnishes for this popular dish: summer, broad beans or favas; fall, simmered bamboo shoots.

*[4 servings]*
1 firm tofu (momen)
1 egg
1–2 Tbsp water
Cornstarch
Cooking oil
1 cup dashi
½ cup light soy sauce
20 broad beans, boiled in salted water
Grated ginger

The dipping sauce has a 2:1 ratio of dashi to soy sauce.

## Prepare the tofu.

1. As shown in step 3 on p. 113, press the tofu until about ⅔ of its original size. Slice into 8 pieces.
• **Wrap well to avoid crumbling.**

2. Beat the egg. Add 1-2 Tbsp water (half as much as the egg).
• **Thinned eggs do not over-adhere to the tofu.**

3. Dip tofu in cornstarch, then in egg.

4. Shake off excess egg and dip in cornstarch again.

## Fry.

5. Heat the oil to 375°F (190°C). When you hear the steam escaping, remove.
• **The tofu will burst if fried too long.**

6. Heat the dashi and soy sauce. Spoon around the tofu and serve with broad beans and grated ginger.

Estimating temperature without a thermometer; and keeping the oil clear while cooking.

### Temperature

**One drop batter.**
• Proper temperature (360°F; 180°C): sinks and floats right back up.
• Too low. Sinks to the bottom; floats up after a moment.
• Too high. Cooks before sinking.

**Sprinkle flour.**
• Proper temperature (360°F; 180°C): sizzles on contact.
• Too low: Makes no sound.
• Too high: Scatters and burns (smoke).

### Cleaning the oil
• Scoop out the remaining fried batter after each batch or it will burn in the oil.
• Stir well with chopsticks to release small bubbles of air and steam. If they stay, they will make the oil taste stale.

# Mackerel Crisps

Dust with flour just before frying, for maximum crispness.

Frying soy-sauce marinated meat or fish after dredging with flour is called *tatsuta-age.* Delicious even when cold, this dish is good for bento boxes or picnics.

*[4 servings]*
1 mackerel in 2 boneless fillets (p. 90)
⅓ cup soy sauce
⅓ cup sake
Pastry flour
Prepared hot mustard

**Slice and soak.**

1. Remove the stomach bones.

2. Pull out the small bones.

3. Slice into bite-size slanted pieces.
•**The marinade makes the fish burn easily. Cut for fast cooking.**

4. Marinate for 15–20 min.

5. Drain on paper towels.

**Fry.**
6. Heat the oil until it makes flour sizzle. Dredge the fish in flour and fry.
•**Pastry flour fries up lighter than cornstarch.**

7. When golden, serve, with the mustard.

The flour becomes sticky if it remains on the fish too long. Fry immediately after dredging.

•**Do not overcook or the mackerel will dry out.**

# Two-Flavor Pan-Grilled Yakitori

Cook uncovered for a crisp finish.

*[8 skewers]*
1 chicken thigh
1 naganegi or 2 scallions
Grilling Sauce (right)
Salt
Cooking oil
Lemon
Shichimi togarashi (seven-spice powder)

## Skewer.

1. Trim and dice the thigh. Cut naganegi or scallions into 1 in (3 cm) lengths.

2. To prevent injury, hold the pieces on the cutting board and skewer them without picking them up. Keep the thickness of the pieces equal. Alternate ingredients.

### Sauced yakitori.

3. Fry 4 skewers in a little oil until one side is fully golden. Turn and cook the other side.

4. Press with a chopstick. If firm, the chicken is done.

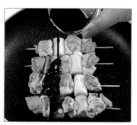

5. Lower heat. Coat in sauce. Garnish with spice powder.

### Salted yakitori.

6. After step 2, sprinkle the remaining 4 skewers well with salt. Follow steps 3 and 4. Garnish with lemon slice.

## Grilling Sauce

Use for Yakitori, Yellowtail Teriyaki (p. 83), and Salmon Teriyaki (p. 84)

*[for 1 cup]*
1 cup soy sauce
1 cup mirin

1. Bring soy sauce and mirin to a boil. Measure depth.

2. Float a plate on top. Cook until tiny bubbles form in the liquid.

3. Spoon off the foam. Cook until depth measures half of the original.

*Pour into a jar, let cool, and store in freezer. It will not freeze solid. When you run low, do not use up the last bit—add to the new batch.

# Seared Beef

Use plenty of salt and pepper-the surface be almost white. The excess will be rinsed off.

Use very fresh beef for this dish. Marinated onion complements nicely.

*[4 servings]*
14 oz (400 g) boneless beef round
Salt
Dash pepper
2 onions
2 cloves garlic
1 cup rice vinegar
⅔ cup soy sauce
⅓ cup sake
Cooking oil
Roasted sesame seeds
Hot mustard
Red leaf lettuce

•The marinade ratio is 3:2:1 vinegar to soy sauce to sake.

**Season the beef.**
1. Cut the meat into blocks 1 x 2 in (3 x 4.5 cm). Salt until the surface looks whitish. Add pepper.

2. Knead to press the salt into the meat.

**Sear the beef.**

3. Fry the beef. Be sure each side is well browned before turning.
•**For best flavor, do not turn over and over. Use high heat for rare; low heat to cook through.**

4. When all sides are browned, plunge in ice water to stop the cooking. Rinse off the browned bits. Dry on paper towels.

**Marinate.**

5. Thinly slice onion and garlic. Combine with the vinegar, soy sauce, and sake.

The extra salt makes the beef last longer also. Refrigerate in marinade 3-4 days without slicing.

6. Marinate beef until the onion is soft (1 hr +). Slice. Serve with sesame seeds, lettuce, onion, and mustard.

# Golden Shrimp

The salt and sake lend a clean flavor to the shrimp.

The egg makes a golden coating. Try this method with other quick-cooking foods, such as scallops or chicken tenderloins.

*[4 servings]*
8 prawns
3 Tbsp sake
½ tsp salt
Pastry flour
2 eggs
8 Japanese sweet peppers
2 Tbsp cooking oil plus more for deep frying

**Trim the prawns.**

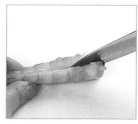

1. Peel the prawns, leaving the tail on. Slice open (slicing through the tail).

2. Remove the vein. The black vein contains eggs and can be left in.

3. Marinate 5-10 min. in salted sake.

4. Pat dry.

**Cook prawns.**

5. Dust with the flour. Heat half the oil. Dip 4 prawns in the egg and place in the hot pan.

6. Cook over low heat until golden on both side. Hold down to cook all sides.

The salt and sake flavor the prawns and erase their odor. This technique can be applied to other seafood also.

7. Repeat with the remaining 4 prawns. Trim the sweet peppers and cut a slit. Deep fry without batter.

# Chapter 7

# Light and flavorful Salads and Cold Dishes

These refreshing dishes complement any meal and, in the case of the quick pickles, can be made ahead to have on hand whenever an extra dish is needed. Experiment with different seasonal vegetables, too.

*Left to right:* Squid and Asparagus; Sesame Pork; Parsley Chicken

## Squid and Asparagus *(photo: p. 108)*

This dish bursts with contrasts. It also works beautifully with udo in place of the asparagus.

*[4 servings]*
7 oz (200 g) squid for sashimi (mongo ika)
1 stalk asparagus
4 Tbsp flying fish roe
2 Tbsp light soy sauce
1 Tbsp boiled sake*
3 Tbsp citrus vinegar or juice
Pinch sugar
1 Tbsp dashi
Salt
*Boiled sake is sake that has been brought to a boil and removed from heat.

**Slice.**
1. Slice at an angle into ¼ in (5 mm) thick slabs.

2. Trim asparagus. Blanch in salted water. Fan to cool.

Cut into 2 in (4.5 cm) lengths.
· **Boil before slicing for best flavor. Cooling in water leads to sogginess.**

**Make marinade.**

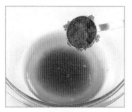

3. Combine all other ingredients except salt. Stir in the roe.

**Combine.**

4. Add the squid. Vinegar gives raw squid a crisp flavor.
5. Add the asparagus and serve.

## Chicken and Parsley *(photo: p. 109)*

This dish is best with seri, a Japanese parsley, but Italian parsley works well also. Use very fresh chicken, or try substituting with squid sashimi or raw oysters.

*[4 servings]*
5 chicken tenderloins
1 bunch seri or Italian parsley
Citrus vinegar or juice
½ cup soy sauce
⅓ cup (scant) boiled mirin (p. 120)
Sesame oil

*If orange vinegar is unavailable, use the sanbaizu from opposite page. Let boil and cool.

· This ponzu uses the sanbaizu ratio. Vinegar-soy sauce-mirin 5:5:3.

**Boil the chicken.**

1. Shake each tenderloin in boiling water until the surface is white. Plunge in ice water.

2. When cool, pat dry with paper towels and slice into slanted slabs.

**Chop parsley.**
3. Refresh parsley in cold water. Drain. Chop into 2 in (5 cm) lengths.

**Make dressing.**
4. Combine the liquids. Use up to half again as much sesame oil.

**Combine.**
5. Gently fold in the parsley, then the chicken. Serve.

# Sesame Pork *(photo: p. 109)*

If vinegared dishes taste too sharp to you, you should definitely try this one. The flavor is almost buttery. The secret? Boiling the vinegar beforehand.

*[4 servings]*
7 oz (200 g) thinly sliced pork loin
5 Tbsp rice vinegar
5 Tbsp light soy sauce
3 Tbsp mirin
3 Tbsp roasted sesame seeds
2 onions, sliced thin
4 shiso leaves

•The vinegar mixture, *sanbaizu*, has a soy sauce-vinegar-mirin ratio of 5:5:3.

**Cook the pork.**

1. Swirl each piece of pork in shivering water until cooked. Plunge in ice water.
•**Cook one at a time to avoid raw spots.**

2. Dry on paper towels. Cut to ½ in (1.5 cm)-wide strips.

**Make dressing.**
3. Heat vinegar, soy sauce, and mirin to boiling. Immediately place pot in cold water. Stir to cool.

4. Crush the sesame seeds lightly—some stay whole—in a grinding mortar. Add the vinegar mixture.

## A quick boil smoothes the vinegar.

Stir while cooling, using a wooden spoon or chopsticks, or the mixture will become cloudy.

**Serve.**
5. Soak the onion in water. Drain. Mound at back of plate. Lay the shiso in front, then add pork. Drizzle with the sesame dressing.

•If desired, hot chili oil may be added to the sesame dressing.

JAPANESE FUNDAMENTALS•
**Vinegar Dressings**

Nihaizu (two-flavor dressing)
Rice vinegar-soy sauce-dashi 5:1:1. Combine. Use with seafood.

Sanbaizu (three-flavor dressing)
Rice vinegar-soy sauce-mirin 5:5:3. Combine, boil, and cool. Use with vegetables or meat.

Amazu (sweet vinegar)
Rice vinegar-mirin-salt 1:1:dash. For marinade, just stir. For dressing, boil vinegar and mirin separately before combining.

Ponzu
Rice vinegar → citrus
Use bitter-orange vinegar (daidaizu), citrus vinegar, or citrus juice in place of the rice vinegar in sanbaizu or nihaizu. No boiling.

# Vegetables in White Dressing

Season the vegetables well so that they are not overwhelmed by the full-bodied dressing.

*[4 servings]*
1 pkg konnyaku noodles (devil's-tongue jelly)
½ cup dashi
2 Tbsp mirin
2 Tbsp soy sauce
1 bunch spinach
2 in (5 cm) carrot
½ block firm tofu (momen)
⅔ tsp miso
1½ Tbsp roasted sesame seeds
3 Tbsp sugar
½ Tbsp light soy sauce
½ Tbsp mirin
Salt

### Also Try: Fuki in White Dressing

Roll 3 fuki (butterbur) in 3 Tbsp salt. Cut to fit in pot and boil 3-5 min. Plunge in cold water and peel. Slice into 1 in (7 mm) diagonals. Add white dressing and serve.

**Prepare dressing.**
1. Simmer tofu for 3 min.; do not let the water boil.

# Tofu sopoils quickly. To be safe, preboil before pressing.

2. Cool in many changes of cold water (lukewarm water bruises the tofu).

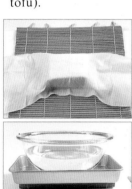

3. When cool, wrap in cloth. Cover with a rolling mat. Weigh down until half size.

4. Press through a strainer into a grinding mortar.

5. Grind well until smooth.

6. Grind in the miso, then sesame, then soy sauce, then mirin. Salt to taste.
•**Order: solids, powders, liquids.**

**Slice vegetables.**
7. Boil the konnyaku from cold water. Drain. Boil again in the dashi, mirin, and soy sauce. Cool in liquid.

8. Drain and chop.

9. Blanch spinach in salted water. Chop to 2 in (5 cm) lengths.

10. Julienne the carrot and boil.

**Combine.**

11. Add konnyaku to the dressing. Squeeze the spinach well and sprinkle in. Add the carrot.

Pressing the tofu takes time. Because it happens at room temperature, heat through beforehand. The dressing will keep longer, too.

12. Stir with a wooden paddle.
•**The paddle will not crush the ingredients.**

## Also Try: Broccoli with Black Sesame Sauce

Blanch broccoli florets in salted water. Drain and cool. Julienne some naruto-maki (fish cake with swirl pattern). Serve with black sesame sauce on the bottom and broccoli and naruto on top.

# Tofu and Pork in Black Sesame Dressing

Keep grinding the sesame until it releases its oil.

This sesame dressing is rich and flavorful. Use a large grinding bowl (suribachi) to make plenty. Briefly re-roasting the sesame before grinding improves the aroma. Also, have someone hold the bowl while you grind—it is easier.

*[4 servings]*
2 oz (60 g) black roasted sesame seeds
1½ Tbsp red miso
6 Tbsp sugar
4½ Tbsp soy sauce
1¼ Tbsp mirin
2 atsuage (thick-fried tofu)
7 oz (200 g) pork loin
5-6 green beans, blanched in salted water

**Make dressing.**

1. Grind the sesame seeds until shiny from releasing oil.

2. Grind in the miso, then the sugar, until thoroughly mixed.

3. Sprinkle the soy sauce and mirin little by little, stirring until smooth.

**Cook tofu, pork.**

4. Swirl aburage in boiling water. On hot days, boil 3 min. to prevent spoiling.

5. Drain in a strainer. Fan to cool.

6. Quarter tofu lengthwise, then cut into ½ in (1.5 cm)-wide strips.

7. Cook, dry, and slice pork as in steps 1 and 2 on p. 111.

8. Cut beans to ¾ in (2 cm) lengths.

When roasted black sesame seeds are ground for a long time, they release their oil as shown here. Put a wet towel under the grinding bowl to protect it.

**Combine.**

9. Fold tofu, pork, and beans into the dressing with wood paddle.

# Round Clams in Miso Dressing

To make the dressing, thin some Miso Sauce *(right)* with vinegar.

*[4 servings]*
4 oz (110 g) round clams, rinsed in salted water
3 shallot greens or scallions
4 Tbsp Miso Sauce *(right)*
1 Tbsp rice vinegar
Prepared hot mustard
Salt

**Boil shallots.**

1. Place shallot greens in boiling water, whites first.

Also Try: Eggplant and Crab in Spicy Miso Sauce

Cut 2 Japanese eggplants into 6 half rounds each. Fry in 375°F (190°C) oil. Cut 4 crab sticks in half. Stir hot mustard into Miso Sauce. Place crab and eggplant on sauce.

2. Boil until the green stalks puff up.
•**They can burst; stand back to avoid burns.**

3. Drain in a strainer. Fan to cool.
•**Do not cool in water: causes sogginess.**

**Combine.**
4. Stir vinegar into Miso Sauce. Mix with round clams and sliced shallots. Serve with mustard.

# Miso Sauce

This handy sauce can be used in miso dressings (with vinegar) or by itself on grilled foods (dengaku).

1 cup miso
1 cup sugar
1 cup mirin

1. Stir the sugar and miso in a pot, using a wooden paddle.

2. Keep mixing until the sugar dissolves and you no longer feel sugar grains.

3. Drizzle the mirin slowly, mixing well.

4. Place on low heat. Stir. Do not let the sauce burn.

5. When the paddle can part the sauce, it has reached the right thickness. Remove from heat. When it stops steaming, seal tightly.
Keeps in refrigerator 2 –3 months.

NOTES: If the miso is coarsely ground (small soybean bits remaining), use up at once. Also, if you use saikyo miso, omit the sugar.

# Japanese-style Crab Salad

Pepper balances the crab-stick flavor.

*[4 servings]*
5 in (12 cm) daikon
5¼ oz (150 g) artificial crab sticks
Scallions
Pinch salt
½ cup mayonnaise
Pepper
Soy Sauce

1. Julienne the daikon.

2. Separate the crab strands and stir in.

3. Knead with salt. Stir in mayonnaise and pepper.

4. Serve with chopped scallions and soy sauce.

# Taro and Tofu Salad

Toasting the bonito flakes is the secret.

*[4 servings]*
6 in (15 cm) taro root (nagaimo)
1 aburage (tofu puff)
1 cup shaved bonito
½ cup kaiware (daikon sprouts)
Rice vinegar
Soy sauce

1. Toast the aburage on a rack until crisp. Oil will be released; avoid burning.

2. Slice lengthwise, then julienne.

3. Julienne the taro and soak in vinegared water. Rinse and drain well.
**The vinegar whitens the taro.**

4. Toast the bonito as shown in step 3, bottom right. Combine aburage, taro, and bonito. To serve, sprinkle with kaiware tops and soy sauce.

# Fava Beans

This dish uses soramame (broad beans) in Japan.

*[4 servings]*
7 oz (200 g) fava beans
½ cup light soy sauce
¾ cup dashi
Salt

1. Slice into the black part of the bean.

2. Boil until tender (2-3 min.) in salted water. Drain.

3. Soak 10 min., skin on, in the soy sauce and dashi *(figure)*.  Drain.

# Ohitashi

Use spinach, mizuna, pea greens, or other tender leafy vegetables for this dish. Toast only as much shaved bonito as you will need—its aroma fades quickly.

*[4 servings]*
1 bunch spinach
Salt
½ cup light soy sauce
¾ cup dashi
Shaved bonito

1. Boil the spinach in salted water. Plunge in cold water.

2. Squeeze well. Cut in half crosswise. Align stems with leaves. Set in dashi and soy sauce.

3. Roast shaved bonito in a pan over very low heat, tossing with your hand *(figure)*. When dry, cool on paper. **•Burns if stirred with chopsticks or if left in pan after turning off.**

4. Sprinkle bonito on chopped spinach.

This refreshing quick pickle is very simple to make. The liquid from the daikon erases the sharpness of the vinegar.

*[4 servings]*
4 in (10 cm) daikon
½ cup rice vinegar
½ cup boiled mirin*
Pinch salt
Roasted black sesame seeds

*Mirin boiled briefly

# Hakusai Quick Pickles

These quick pickles complement any meal. If you do not have a pickle press, just weight with a flat plate.

*[4 servings]*
⅙ head hakusai or napa cabbage
4 in (10 cm) kombu (narrow strip)
1 dried red pepper
Salt

**Knead hakusai.**
1. Chop and weigh the hakusai. Sprinkle with 2% of the weight in salt. Toss gently to soften.
**·To prevent breakage, add force gradually.**

2. Grasp firmly and knead well.

**Pickle.**
3. Julienne the kombu ⅛ in (4 mm) wide. Seed and chop the pepper. Stir both in.

4. Press in a pickle press (or with a plate) for 1 hour. Squeeze well.

*Also tasty with grated citron zest.

**Slice daikon.**
1. Peel and quarter the daikon. Slice very thin.

**Pickle.**
Combine vinegar, mirin, and salt. Stir in the daikon and let stand until soft. Sprinkle sesame.